I GIVE MY HEART

By

Fawn Fulton

Rainbow's End Company
354 Golden Grove Road
Baden, PA 15005

Copyright © 1991
By
Fawn Fulton

"Behold, I will do a new thing; now it shall spring forth; shall ye not know it?" Isaiah 43:19

ISBN: 0-9608780-9-2

DEDICATION

I dedicate this book of poetry to my Heavenly Father, who sent His Son to die for me, took my broken life and my broken heart and put within me His spirit and a new heart that beats only for Him. Without Him I could write nothing of real worth and my life would be empty. Also, I must include in this dedication all those who believed in me and prayed for me in my darkest hours, especially my husband, my best critic.

Edited by:
Judith Blanarik
And
Wayne P. Brumagin

Cover Design by Susan E. Campbell

TABLE OF CONTENTS

LORD,
You
must
be
tired
of
my
trying
TO NAIL YOU TO THE CROSS AGAIN
while
I
kneel
here
whimpering
and
humiliated
by
Your
undying
LOVE.

WHAT IS LOVE?

You asked me
To tell of love.
If you mean love
That seeks her own,
With passions fire
And dewey-eyed discourses
To the beloved,
I cannot.
I can only tell
Of a blood-sprinkled love
Stretched out on a cross,
His body hanging,
Bones pulled from joints,
Lungs crushed
Under the weight
Of my sin,
A beard-plucked,
Thorn-scarred face
Lifted to the Father
Crying, "Forgive them!"
I can tell of that love
For I have looked upon it
And became whole.
Felt its life-changing power.
Impassioned by His love
To love as He loved
Unconditionally,
I give my heart.

APPLES OF GOLD

A wise man once said,
"A picture is worth
A thousand words."
The wisest man said,
"A word fitly spoken
Is like apples of gold
In pictures of silver."

Based on Proverbs 25:11

WHO WILL ANSWER?

Their cries echo through
The aging chambers of my mind
And break the silence
Of life's final fragile rest,
As I drift back to that first call
Of His sweet voice saying,
"Who will answer their cries?"
In my youthful, tender heart
The answer rang, "Lord, here am I;
I will choose the fast
That You have chosen."

No time for sackcloth and ashes
To make my voice heard on high
Nor to think of what might have been
Had I chosen another path.
So little time to answer all the cries,
The endless cries,
"I am the helpless!
I am the abused!
I am the lonely!
I am the lost!"

As time draws the shade upon my life,
Four thousand little faces
Pass before my tired eyes,
And I wait to hear
His sweet voice call once more,
"Well done, thou good and faithful servant,
Enter thou into the joy of thy Lord."

A tribute to Miss Gertrude Ramey, founder of Ramey's Childrens' Home, Ashland, Kentucky, and to all those who unselfishly give their lives to humanity. Miss Ramey, now in her eighties, raised over 4000 children.

FALLEN TEMPLES OF THE STEEL GOD

Your remains rot in deserted courtyards;
While in your sanctuaries
Rusted skeletons of steel-making idols
Stare through hollow eyes
At the broken who pass by,
Living sacrifices burned
On the altars of your hot furnaces,
Sweat sloshing in their shoes
While your steel piled high.
A "Tower of Babel!"
Ingot upon ingot!
Bar upon bar!
Pipe upon pipe!
Poverty and pain your final rewards.
Our spirits cry out,
"Steel, you will no longer be our god!
For you were a false god;
Your ears are deaf to our cries;
Your eyes blind to our miseries!"
Yes, we have learned . . .
We have learned . . .
We must serve the living God!

Written in memory of the steel workers of Beaver Valley

The remains of the J & L Coke Works in West Aliquippa, PA.

A KING IS BORN

Awake! Awake! O' Jerusalem!
Prepare thyself for your King!
Put on your beautiful garments!
Break forth into joy and sing!

Your God reigns forever, O' Zion.
Awake! Your Redeemer is here!
And all the nations of all the earth
Shall see God's salvation appear.

Awake! O' people everywhere!
The Hope of the world has come.
A Light in a world full of darkness,
God's only begotten Son!

Based on Isaiah 52, Luke 1, and John 1.

PROCLAMATION

I will magnify the Lord my God,
Tell of His mercy and grace.
I will love Him with all my heart,
For He has been my hiding place.

I will sing my song upon the mountains
And praise Him in the valleys below,
From everlasting to everlasting
So all the world may know.

Strength and honor are in His sanctuary,
My Loving Father and Everlasting King.
Forever I will abide in the secret place,
Of the Most High God I will sing.

SACRIFICIAL LAMB

Oh, Lamb of spotless white
Before thy shearers still,
Stripped of the glories of Heaven,
To fulfill the Father's will.

Accused, mocked, and beaten,
Nailed naked to the Cross in shame
So all, who would, through the ages
Find salvation in His name.

In the demon chambers of Hell
He conquered death, the grave, and sin,
That He would be the firstfruits
Of all who would live again.

JUST A LITTLE PUPPY

She is just a little puppy
That is longing for her pal,
Who died the death of a hero
In the jungles of Guadalcanal.

The puppy's heart is lonely;
She just can't understand.
All she knows is that she misses
The touch of a gentle hand.

Written in honor of my brother Ben who served in the South Pacific during
World War II. I was 11 years old, and he had given me his puppy to care for
until he returned.

MOTHER'S EYES

My mother's eyes were blue breath's of spring,
The kind that twinkle, laugh, and sing,

Those Jesus-sees-you kind of eyes,
Sometimes stern, but loving and wise.

Eyes that guarded me while I slept,
Strengthened and comforted when I wept.

Memories of mother's eyes still bring
Thoughts of love and joy and spring.

LOST VICTORY

I flipped the words
Off my tongue
With the speed and sting
Of a scorpion.
They hit the mark
Like a well-aimed missile,
Exploding, ripping, tearing,
You crumpled, I ran
To gloat over the kill.
Now you're gone
And I'm alone
To savor the memory
Of my lost victory.

Written to my sister Bette who died in 1979.
I shall always remember an incident that happened when we were young.

BIG SISTER

When you were young,
A little tomboy watched you
With awe and love,
Wanting to touch and squeeze
But you looked so untouchable,
Like a beautiful china doll
That's only meant to be admired.
My heart wanted to reach out,
Take you off the pedestal
And wrestle with you,
Hug you as I did
My old rag doll,
Pull out something, anything
That would show you loved me
Or approved of my loving you,
But I was a coward.
The other night,
As you lay dying,
God performed a miracle of love
In a hardened heart
When a little girl
Clung to you and wept.
The facade vanished;
There was an old rag doll,
Hungry for love.

THE MAN I COULD LOVE

I won't ask you
For silver or gold
Or diamonds or furs;
I only ask you to hold
My hand and pray
And walk with me
Through those dark valleys
I may have to travel,
Or pull me over
A few mountains
When I have no strength
Left to climb,
To be patient
When I'm moody and headstrong,
Be not only my lover
But be my friend.
Love me
When I'm not lovable.
If you can,
Then you're the man
That I could love.

TO MY DAUGHTERS

When you were little,
I'd hold you close
And kiss your fingers
Your piggies, your nose.

Then sit in awe
Of God's grace and perfection
In giving to me
This tiny creation.

It was bottles and diapers
That cluttered the place
But you always could put
A smile on my face.

Then came the dolls,
Play dishes and bears,
The puppy and rabbit
And sleepytime prayers.

Oh! How I dreaded
Those terrible teens
With phone calls and dates
And skin-tight blue jeans.

We had many fights
Over boys and the dishes,
Your not wanting to obey
All of my wishes.

Then sorrows and tears
And drifting apart,
A time for the healing
Of my broken heart.

A time for you
To grow and to see
And turn to the God
Who gave you to me.

Now you're grown
And I'm alone
Longing for the voices
That once filled our home.

I'd happily let you
Clutter the place
For the sound of your voices
Puts a smile on my face.

BECOMING ONE

A sonnet to my husband -- written for our 40th wedding anniversary

As I think back upon our many years,
Through all the days of happiness and pain,
It seems that all the things that caused us tears
Brought forth new growth of life like April rain.
We found becoming one was hard to do,
And days of joy were sometimes far apart,
Learning to separate what's false from true,
I knew you always held me in your heart.
Now, we must live our golden years with grace,
To ravages of time this flesh must bow,
Then on to meet our Savior face to face,
And I will love you then as I do now.
So I shall cherish each remaining day,
For all too quickly life will pass away.

CAN'T

Father,
Without
YOU
I'm a flop
A wet mop
Out of whack
A sad sack
Just a nerd
A lonely bird
Can't love
Need a shove
Can't live
Won't give
Can't win
Lost in sin,
Without
YOU

MARY AND BUD

Her name is Mary;
His name is Bud.
Together we've traveled
A long rough road.
When we were young
We didn't realize
How precious we would become
In each other's eyes.
So we ran
Seeking other friendships,
Other adventures.
Strange how God
Always brought us back
To walk the same road.
Often it would be crooked
And one of us would get
Just around a bend,
A little out of sight.
Somehow the others
Always caught up.
If the road became muddy
With the cares of this life,
And one of us got mired down,
The others pulled or shoved;
Whatever it took.
In the middle of differences
The way sometimes became dry and dusty
But when the dust cleared,
We were all there,
Looking eyeball to eyeball
A little smile
Playing on our faces.
There were times
The road became dark and evil
With Satan lurking in the shadows
To pull us down
With sickness or sorrow or death.
We groped around

For each other's hands
And finding them,
Lifted them to the Father
And like children,
Danced into His light,
"Ring around the rosie,
Pocket full of posie,
Ashes ashes"
No one falls down . . .
When we reach
The end of the road,
It will be with Mary and Bud.

SATAN'S DECEPTION; GOD'S REDEMPTION

He slithered silently into my garden
As an angel of light,
Dangling candy-appled words
Upon my eager appetite.

He said, "If I would partake of this,
Surely God wouldn't keep from me
Promises of eternal bliss
Over one little worldly delicacy."

Beguiled by his charming lies,
I took the fruit like mother Eve.
With visions of becoming wise,
I ate quite sumptuously.

Oh! I became wise alright,
Of lust and greed and pain;
Gone was the spiritual light
Only sorrow and darkness remained.

But God had made a way for me
Through Jesus Christ, His Son.
For on that *Cross* at Calvary
My battle was forever won.

MOUNTAIN MOVER

There is nothing quite as strong,
Though little member it may seem,
As the power of the tongue,
So unruly man can't tame.

But when yielded to the Savior,
Witness of His wondrous love,
Spilling forth the Living Water,
Speaking faith, can mountains move.

THAT GREAT AND GLORIOUS DAWNING

I'm going to see my Savior's face
And have Him smile at me,
While angels' harps strike up a song
To start the jubilee.

The saints that have been waiting
Prepare the banquet hall
For that great and glorious dawning
When I hear the trumpet call.

Be I dead or still yet living,
In the twinkling of an eye,
By His Holy Spirit power
I'll meet Him in the sky.

God Himself shall dry my tears
And take away all pain,
With the Devil out of business
I'll not cry or sorrow again.

I'll put on my robe of righteousness,
Fine linen clean and white,
Never again to walk in darkness
For the Lamb will be my Light.

TRIAL BY FIRE

If the heat of temptation surrounds me
And it seems I'm not going to win,
I'll pray to my Heavenly Father
And find strength and safety in Him.

When the fiery tongues of the wicked
Are picking my life apart,
The Father will be my avenger
For His Spirit dwells in my heart.

Should I stand before kings for my witness
Like the Hebrew children of old,
I'll cry, "My God is able!"
The fire will refine me as gold.

If ever I'm cast into prison
Or being burned at a stake for His name,
I'll look up to the face of Jesus
And reach for His hand through the flame.

TO THE LONELY HEARTS' CLUB

Are you tired and weary and lonely,
Always searching for some goal
To satisfy the deepest longings
Of your soul?
Is it wealth, love, beauty, fame
Or maybe all of these
Make up the game
Of worldly bliss
You think will fill your life
And bring you happiness?
Dear lonely hearts, I beg you see
These baubles will not satisfy.
They are but whispers
In the winds of time
That all too soon
Will pass and die.
Give your lonely heart to Christ
Who brings
Peace and love and all the things
You need to make your very soul to sing.

Christ has died
has risen
will come again

OH, GLORIOUS, HOLIEST, WONDERFUL DAY

When I first met the Savior,
He was hanging on a tree
With nail-pierced hands and a crown of thorns,
And a crowd had come to see.
"Come down! Come down!" I cried,
"Come into the heart of me."
Oh, glorious, holiest, wonderful day,
When Christ came down to me!

The next time that I saw Him
They were placing Him in a tomb.
He was going to the pit of Hell for us,
But the crowd just wandered on home.
"Arise! Arise, my Jesus!
Arise to keep me free!"
Oh, glorious, holiest, wonderful day
When Christ arose for me!

We talked on the way to the city;
He said He wouldn't leave me alone
But would send the Holy Spirit
To keep me 'til He wanted me home.
"Come back! Come back, my Jesus!
Come back to take me with Thee!"
Oh, glorious, holiest, wonderful day,
When Christ comes back for me!

THAT'S WHAT IT'S ALL ABOUT

You aggravate, exasperate,
And drive me to the brink.
Your laziness and immaturity
Make me feel that I will sink.

Then I read a story one has written
That tells me of his pain,
Or look into your eyes and see
Respect and love again.

Suddenly, I hear the voice of God
Down deep inside of me,
"Love them as I've loved you,
For I died to set them free."

And so with mixed up feelings,
I push into your world each day,
Hoping some part of me I'll give to you,
And some part of you I'll take away.

Feelings of the author during her days as a teacher.

I KNOW A PLACE

I know a place where the willows weep
And the wild geese call,
Where the beautiful Ohio runs wide and deep
And the sandy cliffs stand soft and tall.

A tow-headed, lonely child
Ran barefoot on the shore
While her heart raced wild
As she answered the call of the river's lure,

There, she and God frolicked in the sun.
Ever so tightly, He held her hand
As together, laughing, they did run
Through splashing waves upon the golden sand.

NOW I SING A NEW LOVE SONG

I sang the praises of the world
And thought that I was having fun;
Life to me was quite a game.
Old Satan had me on the run.

I searched for pleasure, fame, and wealth,
Used my family and friends,
Living only for myself
To fill the emptiness within.

The game of life that I played,
I just couldn't seem to win
For the Devil always takes his dues
And I was dying in my sin.

Then one day I met a man
Who told me of a love so free,
How God's only Holy Son
Gave His life for you and me.

Now I sing a new love song,
And yes, I walk where I belong.
I sing the praises of the King of Kings;
For He's my life and He's my Song!

MY SACRIFICE

I presented my body
To You, Father,
A living sacrifice
Such as it was,
Scarred by sin
Because of my lust
For things of the world,
Broken and bereaved
Of loved ones
By Satan's cruel hands.
Shattered dreams,
Shattered life
Were all I brought You,
Sorry pieces
Placed on Your altar
But in Your infinite mercy
You said, "That's all I want."

TO THE ADDICT

In my dreams
Your jaundiced, glossy eyes
From sunken sockets
Stare lifeless, pleading
As you hold out
Needle-scarred arms,
Begging for alms, to get a fix
And silence the screaming
In your spirit, soul, and body.

I cry and reach out
To hold and love you,
To tell you of Him
Who died for you
And can put the pieces
Of your life back together.
Then I awake to the reality
That it can only happen
If you really want to be free.

HIS LOVE IS GREAT ENOUGH

My Father's love is great enough
To cause the blind to see,
The lame to walk, the deaf to hear,
And calm a raging sea.

His holy love is great enough
To mend a broken heart,
Heal a mind and light the way
Should we stumble in the dark.

My Father's love is great enough
That He gave His Son for you and me,
To break the bonds of wickedness
And set the captives free.

HIS TRIUMPTH; OUR HOPE

"My God! My **God**!" He cried,
"Why hast Thou forsaken me?"
And gross darkness filled the sky;
The verdict was this Holy Son must die
That man might once again
Find fellowship with God.

With visage marred more than any man,
Bearing our sorrows and pains,
Down from the Father's grace He fell
While all the blackened hounds of Hell
Reached out their ghoulish arms
And caught the Falling Star.

Three long days the battle raged,
Son of God, Son of Man
Held Satan and his fiends at bay
Then on that Resurrection Day,
Broke the chains of sin and death
And rose triumphant from the grave!

THE PRIZE

Winter whips its icy snow
Against the panes,
And I am drifting. . .
Back to West Virginia,
To other winters
Where a young girl
Hungry, shivering
Against the white
Of winter gales,
Climbs the rocky path
To her one-room school
And English class,
A world of dreams
Where poets dwell,
And she stands tall
Among them.
But at 19
Christ came along,
And she set aside
Dreams of self
For the better prize
Of His high calling.

THE COMFORT ZONE

We Christians are too often prone
To serve our God in the comfort zone.
We fast and pray and sing our praises
With lifted hands and angelic faces.
Then it's out the door and head for home
To settle down in our comfort zone.

Out in the streets the homeless are crying.
On beds of affliction many are dying.
Jesus sent us to all the world;
The perimeters of which are not our yard.
We love our church and those at home,
But His love went beyond the comfort zone.

IN THE DIFFICULT HOUR

Lord, fill me
With Your Holy Spirit power,
That in the difficult hour
While racked with pain,
Or pulled apart
By temptation's strain,
I may hold faith fast
And rise to meet You,
Victorious at last!

A FRIENDSHIP BORN

Some friendships are a foreverness
Of building and rebuilding
On foundations of sand they crumble
When storms or the wolf
HUFFS and *PUFFS!*

I like the kind born suddenly
To strangers
When their souls touch
With no fanfare or
Forced formalities

Just silent, warm signals sent
Across spiritual wavelengths
Saying, "I like you."
Message received and returned,
"I like you too."

FOLLOW THE STAR

Have you room for Jesus
In your heart today?
Or will you like others
Just send Him away?

Won't you follow the star
To that Bethlehem town,
To the manger that cradles
God's holy Son?

Kneel at His side
Your life to renew;
Then with the angels
You'll be praising Him too.

Make room in your heart
For Jesus today.
He will save you and love you;
Don't send Him away.

Won't you follow the star
To that Bethlehem town
To the manger that cradles
God's Holy Son?

BEHOLD THE LIGHT

A holy night, a joyous night
When the Christ-Child came to earth.
Immanuel, in Him was life,
And heavenly hosts sang of His birth.

He must be bruised and bear our griefs,
Be despised and rejected of men.
The Light of the World that knew Him not,
While the sins of all were laid on Him.

This Christmas night, behold the Light!
Of a world full of darkness and sin,
For He's the Great Shepherd, the Counselor Divine
Our Healer, Redeemer, and King.

A QUIVER FULL?

Father, far be it from me
To doubt Your Word,
And I know that
"Children are an heritage of the Lord,"
But frankly, I must admit
That "Happy is the man
That has his quiver full of them,"
Stretches my faith quite a bit.

FAITH

Faith, the invisible substance
Of the tangible things
My spirit embraces,
Evidenced through my willingness
To see what is not there.
It is the exceeding abundance
Above all I ask
Or could possibly dream
If I will but yield
To His Holy Spirit power.

GOLF IN HEAVEN?

Lord, I don't know if Your planning
Any golf courses in Heaven
But it sure would be fun.
I can see it now . . .
A foursome scramble;
I get to set up the teams.
You, Paul, Betsy King, and I
Against Peter, Lazarus, Mary, and Martha.
Matthew, Mark, Luke, and John
Can make up the third team.
Lord, You and Betsy take care of the long shots;
Paul and I will handle the chipping and putting.
I sure like that gold putter You gave me.
No, Matthew, you can't collect taxes from your team.
Okay Lord, You have the honors.
Now really, Luke, do we have to holler"fore" up here?
Oops! Is that Peter throwing his driver
Into the river?
And what's Martha doing
Cleaning the green with a broom?
Well, one thing sure
We don't have to worry about it getting dark
Before we get 18 in.
Now Peter, you're not supposed to cry up here;
It's only a game.
Lord, even if there won't be any golf courses
In Heaven,
I still want to be with You.

SUMMERS IN MY HEART

A summer breeze ruffles my hair,
Half-heartedly, I flip the line
Over the side of the boat
And lie back to dream of other summers
With two friends, tanned and smiling,
The four of us racing up the Shenango
To a favorite fishing spot,
Tony at the helm, Bill watching the fish-finder
While you and I stretch out on the bow
Loving the warm sun, the soft breeze,
The feeling of being free for awhile.

How about our first real vacation
When we actually had money for a motel?
We were like four kids
On the greatest adventure of our lives,
Touring Busch Gardens,
Days and nights on Virginia Beach.
Even two days of rain didn't dampen our joy.

The next summer it was Cocoa Beach and Disney World.
We lay on the sand watching puffs of clouds
Like woolly, white sheep
Drift lazily across the sky
And those silly, skinny-legged gulls
Scampering about after food.

Ah! We felt so free and satisfied.
You dragged us on everything
That moved at Disney World;
Except that space mountain thing
And you know who was chicken to get on.
Then I pouted for a Carnival Cruise
That last day.

Our love's been tested too
In the furnace of our hot tempers
And the unbridled tongues of those
Who would destroy what we have.
We've shared so many joys
And pains too.
When no one else understood or seemed to care,
We knew each other's tears and fears.

Time and distance have interfered
With the joy of our being together.
But I thank God for blessing us
With friends who love and accept us
Just the way we are,
Sometimes foolish, sometimes crazy, always late.

MARY'S LAMENT

"Wait Joseph, let me hold Him
One more time
Before you take Him
To the tomb."
Oh, Holy Child of God,
Birthed in my womb,
To see You lying there
Is far too much
For a mother's heart to bear.
I nursed You, my Son,
Held You close and watched You grow,
My precious one,
So innocent and pure
And full of grace.
Your beautiful face . . .
Oh! What have they done
To Your beautiful face?
And Your gentle hands
That touched so many,
How could they have pierced them so?
I knew You were Your Father's
From the beginning
But I didn't want to let You go;
Forgive me, Son,
I don't want to let go now;
Just one last time
I kiss Your brow.
Your Father has told me
There was no other way.
I just want You to know
How proud I was of You today.

I REMEMBER

I remember days spent
High in treetops
Swaying in the wind,
Far from the din
Of fighting siblings
And my father's rantings.

Aloft in my own little world,
I rode magnificent steeds,
Was kissed by valiant
Prince William,
Who lived at the end
Of our lane.

No nightngale's song
Was ever so sweet
As when I sang;
My novels thrilled thousands
While the whole world down there
Cheered and applauded.

In my more melancholy moments
I talked to God
And before I left the heights
Of my solitary place,
I stretched forth my hand
And touched His face.

PRIDE'S PAWN

I invited you in, Jesus,
"Take the whole house,"
I said, "a living sacrifice
Holy, acceptable unto You."

Then pride came calling;
I let him spend the night,
And while he snuggled down
In Your warm bed,
You were shuffled
Quietly into the spare room.
"Oh, he'll be gone tomorrow
And You can have Your room back,"
I promised.
But pride and I got along so well;
He was such good company
That I just couldn't let him go so soon.

I called You for breakfast today . . .
There wasn't any answer . . .
Suddenly,
Pride became a nauseating guest.

LITTLE CREATURES EXCEEDINGLY WISE

The ants are a people not strong at all,
And certainly with brains quite small,
Yet, they gather food all summer long
So they can sing a winter song.

A conie is a folk that's feeble,
Not nearly as smart as people,
But in the rocks he builds his home
Where neither wind nor rain nor flood can roam.

The locusts have no king to lead;
They really are a naughty breed.
Yet, go they forth all in bands,
No matter what, together they land.

The tiny spider majestic stands
Working diligently with her hands,
Spins her web of fancy laces,
Be it in shanties or kingly places.

It's not the brains, the strength, nor the size;
It's the wisdom of God that makes one wise,
And the willingness to do whatever needs done,
The thread of which life's web is spun.

Based on Proverbs 30:24-28

HE DID

Jesus Saves!
The little plaque
On the altar
Said. I wonder
If He will
Me, so ragged
And little and
Insignificant, I
Timidly shuffled
My life forward
Into His big arms
And He did!

RENEWAL

Gray, dying winter
Lays her shroud over the earth
But resurrected spring
Pushes emerald green
Toward the sun
While forsythias pop their buds
In gold array.
All reminding us once more
Of a greater resurrection day
And gives renewed meaning
To being born again.

IF YOU GO AWAY

If you go away,
I'll try not to grieve too long
And do my best
To see the violets and the lilies
In the spring,
Hear the robin's song,
Because they are you.

If you go away,
Summer's sun will still be welcome
At my door.
Sooner or later I will feel
An ocean breeze
Or smell a rose once more,
Because they are you.

If you go away,
The splendor of crimson and gold
Will return in the fall.
I'll look up when I hear
The wild geese call
As of old,
Because they are you.

If you go away,
Still, winter's white will clothe the pine;
The open hearth still burn.
While redbirds flit
From tree to fence,
My lonely heart will yearn,
Because they are you.

His precious blood ran down
Over the mercy seat
And splashed on the whole world
While the Father crowned Him King.

While the willows weep
The sun sinks low in the West;
Tide waters wash sand.

Mr. Moon peeps around,
The warm nights bring out blossoms
For the bumblebees.